SOLDIER

Jim Winchester

An Hachette UK Company
www.hachette.co.uk

First published in Great Britain in 2014 by Ticktock,
an imprint of Octopus Publishing Group Ltd
Endeavour House
189 Shaftesbury Avenue
London
WC2H 8JY
www.octopusbooks.co.uk
www.ticktockbooks.co.uk

ISBN 978 1 84898 928 3
A CIP record for this book is available from the British Library

Printed and bound in China

1 3 5 7 9 10 8 6 4 2

Editor: S Beard Designer: David Freeland
Publisher: Tim Cook   Managing Editor: Karen Rigden   Senior Production Manager: Peter Hunt
Picture Researcher: Jim Winchester

SOLDIER

Ticktock

CONTENTS

TRAINING & TECHNIQUES

PERSONNEL & EQUIPMENT

ARMIES, NAVIES & AIR FORCES

Almost every nation has armed forces. While they may defend a country's territory and back up its foreign policy, they can also help after disasters, operate with allies and perform peacekeeping missions to prevent further conflict.

ARMIES

Wars usually need personnel at the scene – "boots on the ground" – to capture and hold territory before a political solution can be achieved. In battle, the infantry soldier has the support of artillery, tanks and attack helicopters. Army vehicles and transport helicopters bring rations and ammunition, and also take the wounded to hospital.

AIR FORCES

Most air forces operate fighters, bombers, cargo transporters, surveillance aircraft, trainers and larger helicopters. Some also have responsibility for long-range ground-launched missiles and satellites. Air defence and sudden long-range attacks are air forces' specialities.

NAVIES

Keeping sea lanes open for trade - by hunting submarines, destroying mines, fighting pirates and catching smugglers - is just one of the roles naval forces have in both war and peace. Long endurance combined with sophisticated electronics, weapons and their own aircraft allow fleets to patrol vast areas of ocean.

INFANTRY

The humble foot soldier or infantryman is the core of any army. A typical infantry platoon or squad consists of several riflemen plus specialists with a variety of support weapons, led by an NCO or junior officer.

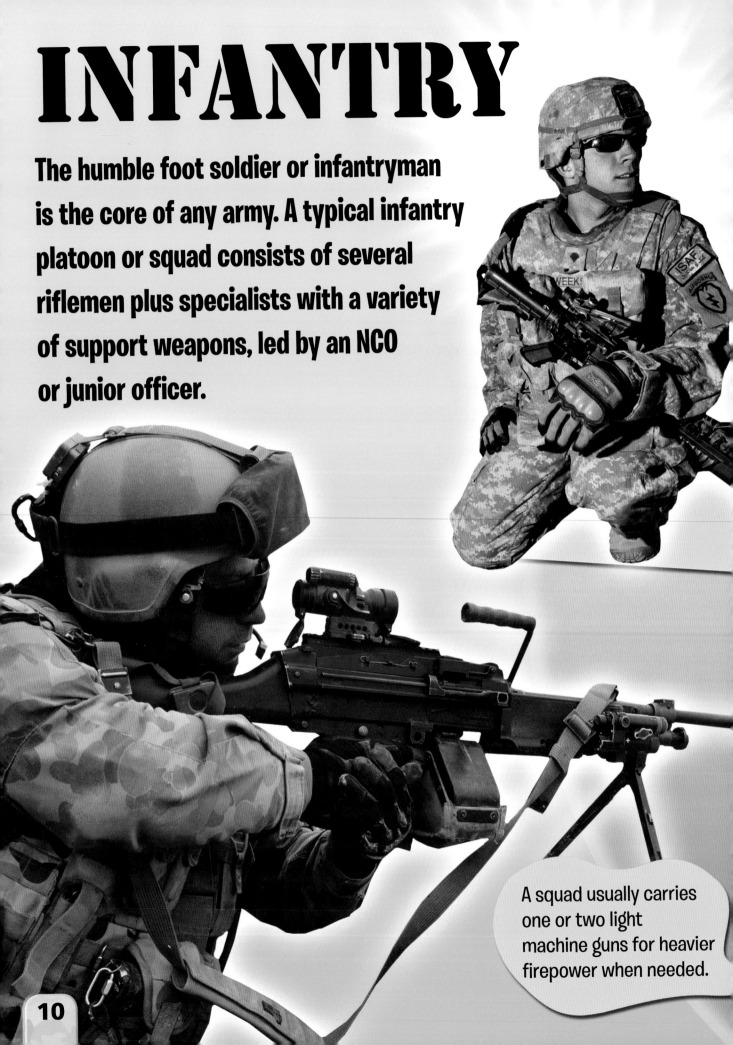

A squad usually carries one or two light machine guns for heavier firepower when needed.

BOOTS ON THE GROUND

Even with today's satellite and drone technology, to win wars the infantryman must cover the terrain, prepare food and shelter and engage the enemy face to face. It has been this way for hundreds of years.

RIFLEMAN

The modern infantry rifleman is well equipped, but must be fit! His rifle, body armour, ammunition, grenades, radio, medical kit, rations and other gear together weigh about 80lb (36kg).

MORTAR CREW

Mortars are a kind of portable artillery commonly used by infantry units. They fire explosives, illuminating flares or smoke markers at a high angle when the bomb is dropped into the tube.

MARINES

Marines specialise in landing troops ashore and supporting them with their own aeroplanes, helicopters, tanks and artillery. Many nations have marine units, but the US Marine Corps (USMC), whose motto is *Semper Fidelis* ("Always Faithful"), is by far the largest and best equipped.

A FEW GOOD MEN

All US Marines start off with a tour as an infantry rifleman. That way they understand the needs of the "grunts" on the ground even if they then train as fighter pilots, tank crews or in other specialities.

HARRIER

The USMC's aviation branch is bigger than many foreign air forces. The most famous Marine aircraft today is the AV-8B Harrier fighter and attack jet. Able to take off and land vertically, it can land on smaller ships or at a landing pad near the battlefield.

HOVERCRAFT FULL OF WHEELS

The LCAC (Landing Craft, Air Cushion) is a large hovercraft that can take troops or vehicles such as these from a ship at sea to the landing beach. Hovercraft move fast and can operate in very shallow water or on land.

IS IT A BIRD?

The extraordinary V-22 Osprey is a tiltrotor – a hybrid aeroplane and helicopter. The US Marines use it as a troop transporter that can go as fast as a cargo plane but land in a small space.

SPECIAL FORCES

Special Forces are the best-trained and equipped troops, and are given the most dangerous missions, such as raids, long-range patrols and counter-terrorist operations. The US Navy SEALs, US Army Delta Force and Britain's Special Air Service regiment are all SF units.

Training together, SF soldiers from several nations show a wide variety of personal equipment.

HIGH JUMP

HALO – High Altitude, Low Opening – is a parachuting technique used on many SF missions. Jumping from a high-flying aircraft, the soldiers will free fall a long way before opening their chutes. (On real missions it is usually done at night.)

ALL THE GEAR

Special Forces often choose their own weapons and equipment, getting gear that's not standard issue. They are also sometimes allowed to have beards and haircuts that don't look very military!

SEALS IN THE WATER

With a name that comes from SEa, Air and Land, the US Navy SEALs specialise in boat and parachute raids against coastal targets or on ships. In a recent mission, an American oil tanker was recaptured from pirates off Somalia.

15

ARTILLERY

Artillery is known as "The King of the Battlefield", because its destructive power can be delivered anywhere. Modern artillery guns (also called howitzers) can fire shells so far over hills and mountains that soldiers at the gun position (called the battery) can't see where they land.

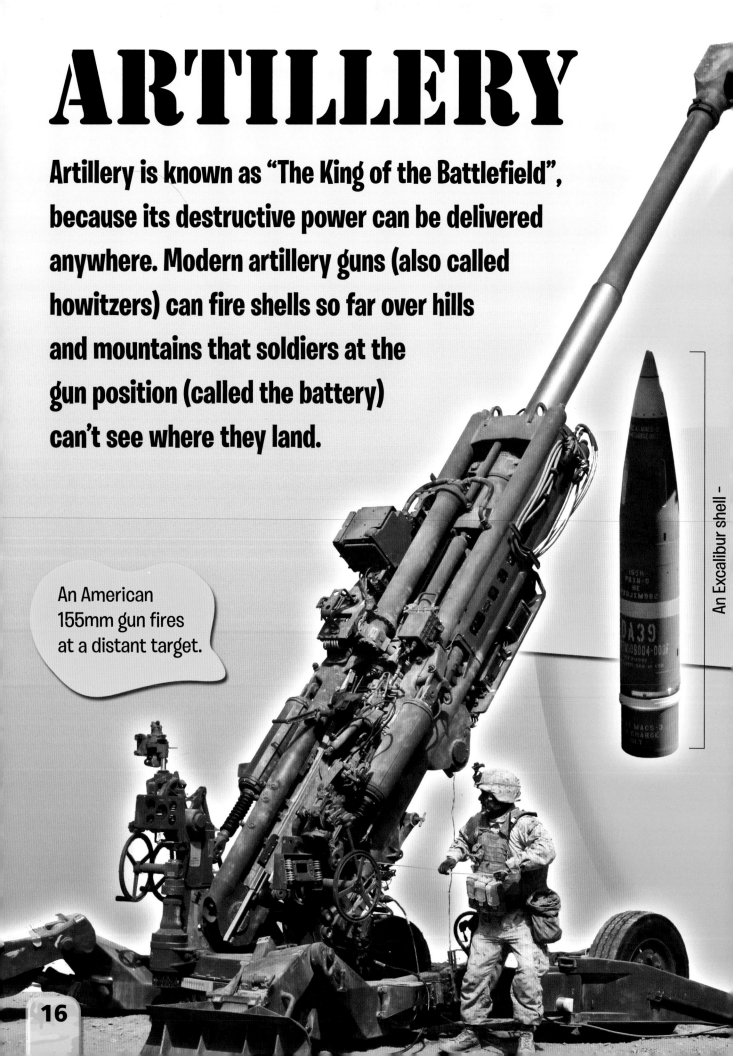

An American 155mm gun fires at a distant target.

An Excalibur shell –

LIGHT GUN

A gun's calibre is the size of the hole at the end of its barrel. This British gun is 105mm calibre, and it can fire about 22,500yds (20km). It's small enough to be towed by light trucks or lifted by helicopters to its firing position.

TARGETED BOOM

Long-range guns such as this 155mm use guided shells, which make a hit much more likely. One new type of guided shell is called Excalibur (after the legendary sword of King Arthur). GPS satellite guidance helps it to hit the target precisely. It can be fired up to 25 miles (40.2km), with an accuracy of within 16ft (4.9m) at shorter ranges. They are much more expensive than ordinary rounds - each Excalibur shell costs over $50,000.

ARTILLERY SPOTTER

The first shells fired are often a little off the target. The artillery spotter or observer watches where they fall and radios back corrections so the battery can adjust its fire.

PARATROOPER

Paratroopers are specialised soldiers who parachute into action. They carry all the gear they need to fight until heavier forces arrive. They often have to secure airfields and capture important objectives such as bridges.

An American 82nd Airborne Paratrooper.

Helmet

Parachute harness

Static line

Ripcord handle

Padded equipment bag

T-10 main parachute

T-10R reserve parachute

Battledress uniform

Boots

GERONIMO!

It takes courage just to get to the action. Paratroopers can jump from many types of aeroplane or helicopter. A static line attached to the aircraft pulls the parachute open, but if that doesn't work, there's always a reserve chute.

CHUTE DESCENT

Military parachutes are round and larger than civilian sport chutes. This makes them harder to steer but able to lower heavier loads gently to the ground. Heavy equipment can be hung below the paratrooper to lessen the bump on landing.

DROP ZONE

When the paratrooper hits the ground there's no time to relax. They must pack up their chute, ready their weapons and find their comrades before the real action begins.

TANK CREW

Tank crew or "tankers" work in a cramped space. Their tank is also their home and needs a lot of looking after. Close cooperation is essential to manoeuvre the tank and use its weapons effectively. On the M1 Abrams and other modern tanks, electronic systems help the crew shoot accurately and stay in battle formation.

COMMANDER

The tank commander tells the rest of the crew what to do and communicates with other tanks by radio. He also operates one of the machine guns mounted on the turret roof.

GUNNER

The gunner sits on the right of the turret. He aims the main gun using an electronic sight or a thermal imaging sight, chooses the ammunition type and fires the gun when the commander gives the order.

DRIVER

The driver's position is the most cramped. He sits in a reclined seat just below the main gun and uses handlebars to steer the tank and a twist grip to speed up. When the tank is "buttoned up", the only view is through a periscope.

LOADER

The loader picks the ammunition from a rack and feeds it into the gun. He calls "Up!" when the shell is loaded. He also fires a machine gun mounted on top of the turret by his hatch.

M1 ABRAMS TANK

The M1 Abrams is America's main battle tank. Used by the US Army and Marine Corps, and by several other armies around the world, it has excellent firepower, protection and mobility.

Commander's 0.5in machine g

Commander's hatch

Communications antennae

Turret basket containing spare equipment

Spare track links

Drive wheel

M1 ABRAMS TANK FACTS

Jet power
The M1 is powered by a 1,500 horsepower gas turbine engine.

Heavyweight
The 70-ton Abrams can do 42mph (67.6km/h) on the road.

See in the dark
A thermal imaging sight sees at night and through fog, smoke and sand clouds.

Gas guzzler
The M1 uses 60 gallons (273 litres) of fuel each hour - that's 0.6 miles per gallon!

Make tracks
The M1 has a ground pressure about half that of the average car.

Big gun
The 120mm gun can destroy another tank up to 2,500yds (2.3km) away.

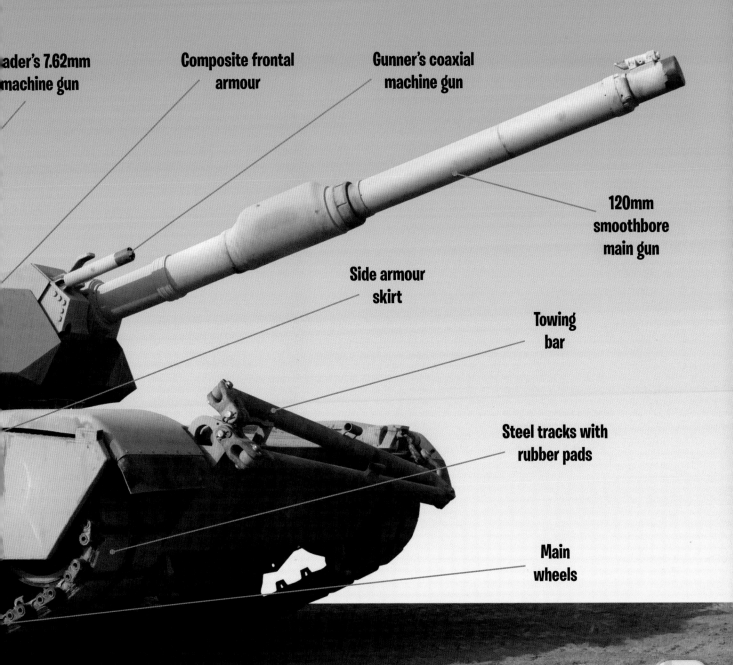

Loader's 7.62mm machine gun

Composite frontal armour

Gunner's coaxial machine gun

120mm smoothbore main gun

Side armour skirt

Towing bar

Steel tracks with rubber pads

Main wheels

COMBAT MEDIC

When a soldier is wounded, combat medics rush in to give first aid. These medics provide all essential medical services, and can sometimes come to the aid of civilians too. If the injuries are serious the soldier needs "medical evacuation" - medevac - to a field hospital.

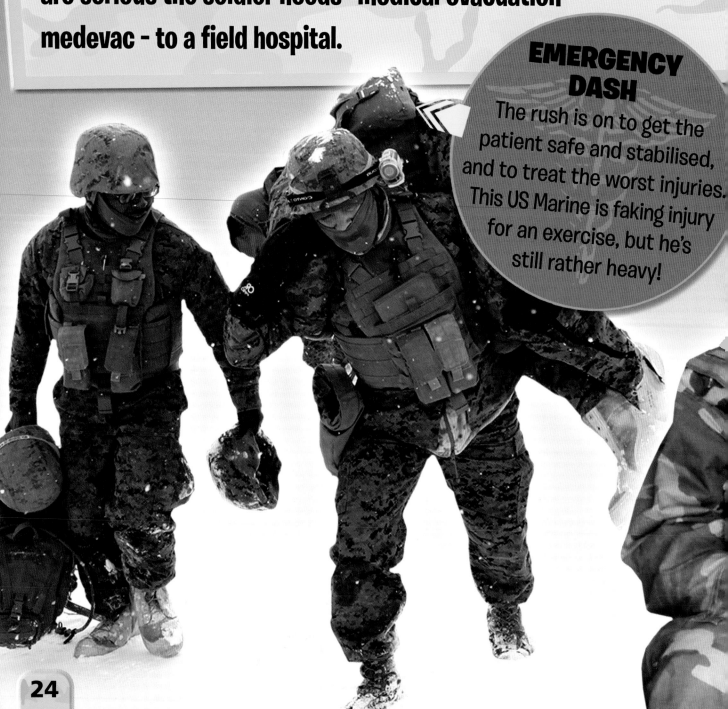

EMERGENCY DASH

The rush is on to get the patient safe and stabilised, and to treat the worst injuries. This US Marine is faking injury for an exercise, but he's still rather heavy!

MEDEVAC CHOPPER

This US Blackhawk helicopter can get the wounded to hospital within the "golden hour" when survival chances are the best. It carries extra medical kit and a doctor.

OUCH!

When not in combat, medics treat routine medical problems and accidental injuries. They also give flu jabs and other shots. Even tough soldiers don't like needles!

HELPING THE PEOPLE

In war-torn countries and places hit by natural disaster, locals need treatment too. The medics can help when local doctors, clinics or hospitals can't cope or don't exist.

TRUCK DRIVER & SUPPLY TROOPS

Hauling everything from bombs and bullets to letters and beans, truck drivers keep an army going. Moving supplies, ammunition and fuel to where it's all needed is called logistics, and it's just as important as battle tactics.

89 KH 02

CONVOY
Travelling together gives mutual protection and allows a lot of trucks to pass in a short time. A convoy can be several miles long and contain everything from fuel tankers to armoured personnel carriers.

EYES ON THE ROAD

The truck driver's job requires skill and concentration. He or she must deal with bad roads, damaged bridges, rough terrain, missing signs and enemy attacks, mostly in "softskin" trucks with little protection.

LOOK, NO HANDS!

The British and US Armies use loading systems that let drivers load and unload massive containers without getting out of their cabs. Trucks can stop, pick up 16-ton loads and drive away in under a minute.

TOP COVER

The supplies must get through, so a gunner scans the roadside for potential ambushes and hidden bombs, and keeps civilian traffic at a safe distance.

MASTIFF MRAP TRUCK

This six-wheel drive armoured truck is a Mine-Resistant Ambush-Protected vehicle - MRAP for short. It's built to keep its occupants safe from mines, bombs, rockets and other threats.

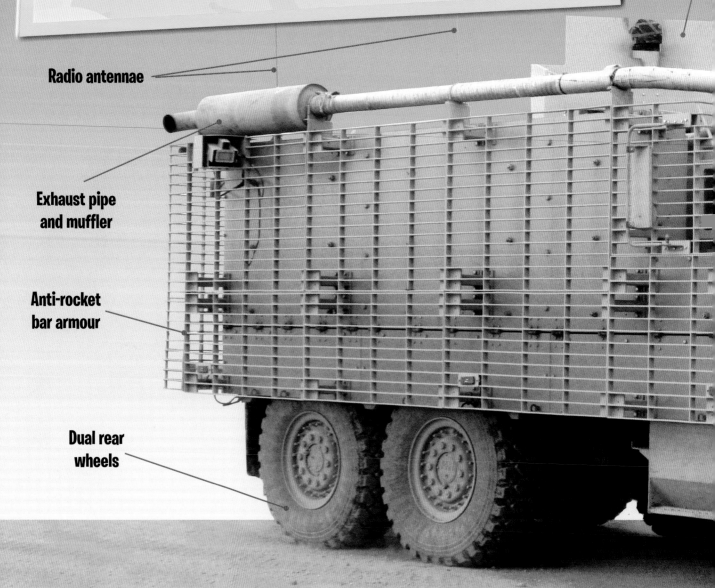

Machine
shield

Radio antennae

Exhaust pipe
and muffler

Anti-rocket
bar armour

Dual rear
wheels

MASTIFF MRAP TRUCK FACTS

Cool cabin
The cabin is air-conditioned and pressurised to keep out chemicals and radioactive particles.

No flats
The tyres are designed to re-inflate if punctured and self-extinguish if on fire.

Behind bars
A cage-like armour system detonates rockets before they strike the MRAP itself.

Road warrior
Power steering, air brakes and a push-button automatic gearbox make driving the 19-ton truck easy.

Top gun
Machine guns or grenade launchers can be fitted to the roof.

Blast protection
The underside is V-shaped to deflect the force of an explosion.

Overhead-wire cutters

Armoured-glass windshield

Protected equipment

330 horsepower diesel V8 engine

Bomb jammer

Run-flat tyres

FF 27 AB

FORWARD AIR CONTROLLER

The Forward Air Controller (FAC), sometimes called a Joint Tactical Air Controller (JTAC), travels with the infantry and calls in air strikes when needed. The Controllers are usually air force soldiers, specially trained to describe target locations to pilots so they can pick them out from the air.

CLEARED HOT!

An A-10 jet streaks over the FAC's position. When "cleared hot", the pilot is authorised to use his weapons. Sometimes weapons aren't needed, and a low and fast "show of force" by a jet will make the enemy change his mind about attacking.

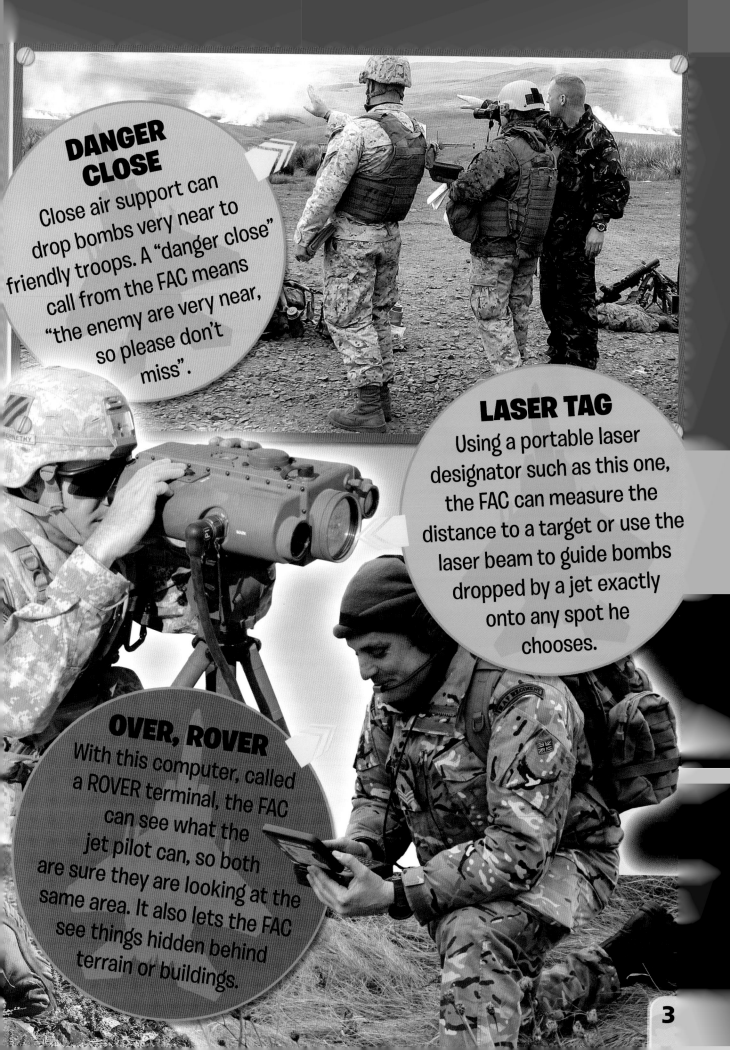

DANGER CLOSE

Close air support can drop bombs very near to friendly troops. A "danger close" call from the FAC means "the enemy are very near, so please don't miss".

LASER TAG

Using a portable laser designator such as this one, the FAC can measure the distance to a target or use the laser beam to guide bombs dropped by a jet exactly onto any spot he chooses.

OVER, ROVER

With this computer, called a ROVER terminal, the FAC can see what the jet pilot can, so both are sure they are looking at the same area. It also lets the FAC see things hidden behind terrain or buildings.

AH-64D APACHE ATTACK HELICOPTER

Used by the US Army and many allied forces, the Apache is the most sophisticated attack helicopter in service. Its highly advanced Longbow radar and sensors allow the crew to attack and destroy multiple targets with cannon, rockets or Hellfire missiles.

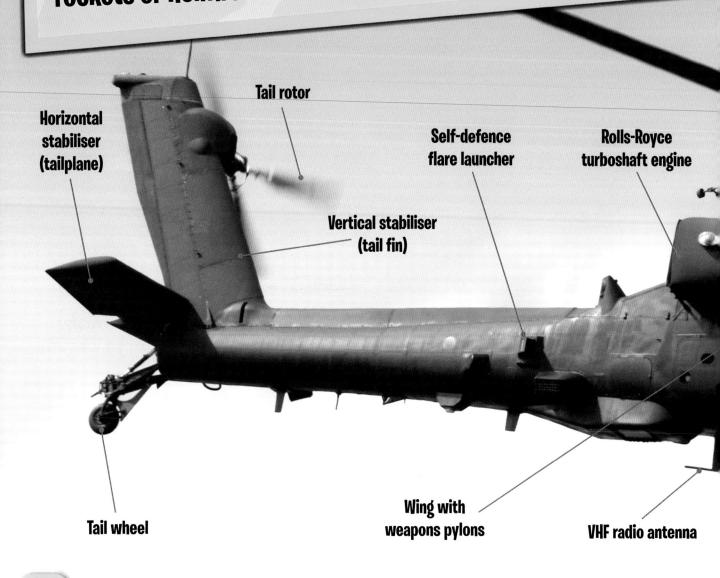

Tail rotor

Horizontal stabiliser (tailplane)

Self-defence flare launcher

Rolls-Royce turboshaft engine

Vertical stabiliser (tail fin)

Tail wheel

Wing with weapons pylons

VHF radio antenna

AH-64D APACHE ATTACK HELICOPTER FACTS

I see you!
The Longbow radar can detect and recognise 256 targets in a few seconds.

Folded away
The rotor blades on British Apaches can be folded back so they can be carried aboard ships.

Look and shoot
Using a sight mounted on his helmet, either crewman can aim the cannon just by turning his head.

Royal ascent
Britain's Prince Harry served as an Apache pilot with the Army Air Corps in Afghanistan.

Hide and peek
Putting the radar up high lets the Apache hide behind trees and terrain, and view the battlefield undetected.

Flying tank
The vital areas of the Apache, such as the cockpit and fuel tanks, are protected by Kevlar composite armour.

Longbow radar dome

Main rotor blades

Pilot's station

Co-pilot/gunner's station

Armoured windscreen

Pilot's Night Vision System and Direct View Optics Sensor

Air-to-ground rocket pod

Fixed main undercarriage

Armoured cockpit sides

30mm chain gun cannon

MINE CLEARANCE & BOMB DISPOSAL

Land mines and improvised explosive devices (IEDs) are a great threat to soldiers on the ground. Mine detectors and dogs help find the devices which must then be made safe by bomb disposal specialists. These men and women have one of the most dangerous jobs in the world.

SAFE DETONATION

Canadian soldiers detonate explosives they found in an Afghan village. In Afghanistan the main danger to soldiers and civilians is from IEDs, and destroying bomb factories is an important mission.

MINE DETECTOR

The metal in a mine or bomb will set off a noise in the headset of a metal detector, but sometimes mines are made mostly of plastic to avoid detection. A path must be swept before troops can cross an area where there might be hidden mines.

They need to do their job perfectly. One mistake could be disastrous.

BOMB SUIT

The MK5 Bomb Disposal Suit weighs 57lbs (26kg) and the helmet 10lbs (4.5kg) or more. It has a fan inside for cooling and a built-in radio, but it's still hot and uncomfortable, and makes hearing difficult.

MILITARY POLICE

Military police officers - MPs - enforce military laws, which are often tougher than civilian laws. MPs work with the normal police to patrol bases, run checkpoints, train MPs from allied armed forces, keep military personnel safe when off base, and investigate crimes involving military personnel.

DOG WATCH

This Dutch MP has a great sidekick - a military working dog. Dogs are used to patrol bases, provide airfield security and search for smuggled material such as drugs or explosives.

CAUGHT AND CUFFED

The Marine in cuffs was found to have illegal drugs in his room and so is being arrested by MPs. If found guilty he can expect a lon sentence in a military prison.

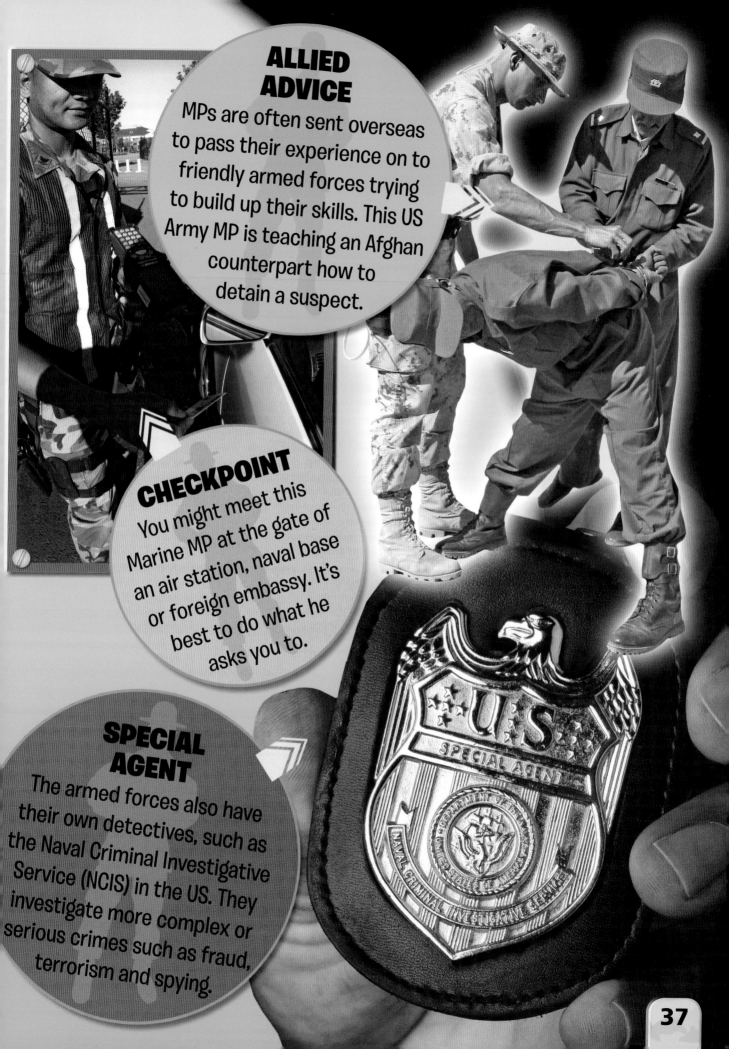

ALLIED ADVICE

MPs are often sent overseas to pass their experience on to friendly armed forces trying to build up their skills. This US Army MP is teaching an Afghan counterpart how to detain a suspect.

CHECKPOINT

You might meet this Marine MP at the gate of an air station, naval base or foreign embassy. It's best to do what he asks you to.

SPECIAL AGENT

The armed forces also have their own detectives, such as the Naval Criminal Investigative Service (NCIS) in the US. They investigate more complex or serious crimes such as fraud, terrorism and spying.

SAILOR

Whatever the size and type of their ship, each sailor has a vital role. In warfare, everyone has a battle station, be it controlling a weapons system, navigating, or standing by to repair damage; the rest of the time, there's always maintenance to be done.

CAPTAIN'S CALL

The ship's captain is responsible for everything that happens on board, including the welfare of the crew and the smooth running of its weapons and equipment.

HOIST THE FLAGS

Even with modern communications systems, flag signals still have their uses. Coloured flags are a fail-safe way of telling nearby ships what this warship is doing.

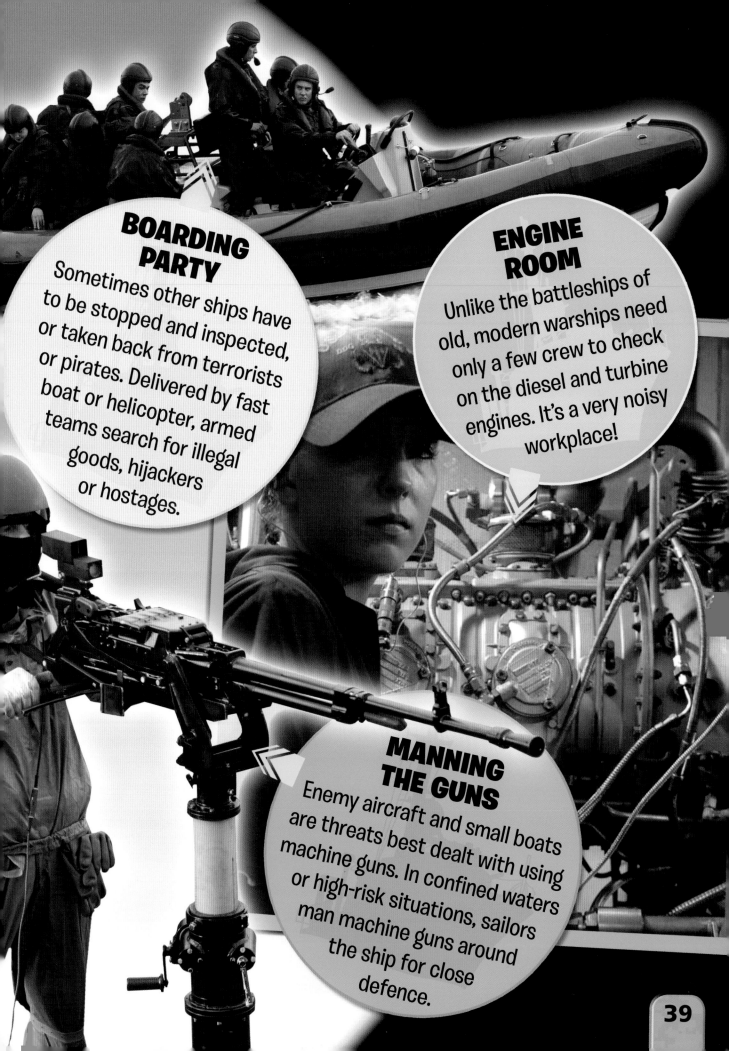

BOARDING PARTY

Sometimes other ships have to be stopped and inspected, or taken back from terrorists or pirates. Delivered by fast boat or helicopter, armed teams search for illegal goods, hijackers or hostages.

ENGINE ROOM

Unlike the battleships of old, modern warships need only a few crew to check on the diesel and turbine engines. It's a very noisy workplace!

MANNING THE GUNS

Enemy aircraft and small boats are threats best dealt with using machine guns. In confined waters or high-risk situations, sailors man machine guns around the ship for close defence.

TYPE 45 DESTROYER

The British Royal Navy's Type 45 destroyer is the most advanced surface warship in the world. It can defend a fleet against air attack, destroy targets ashore and support a landing force.

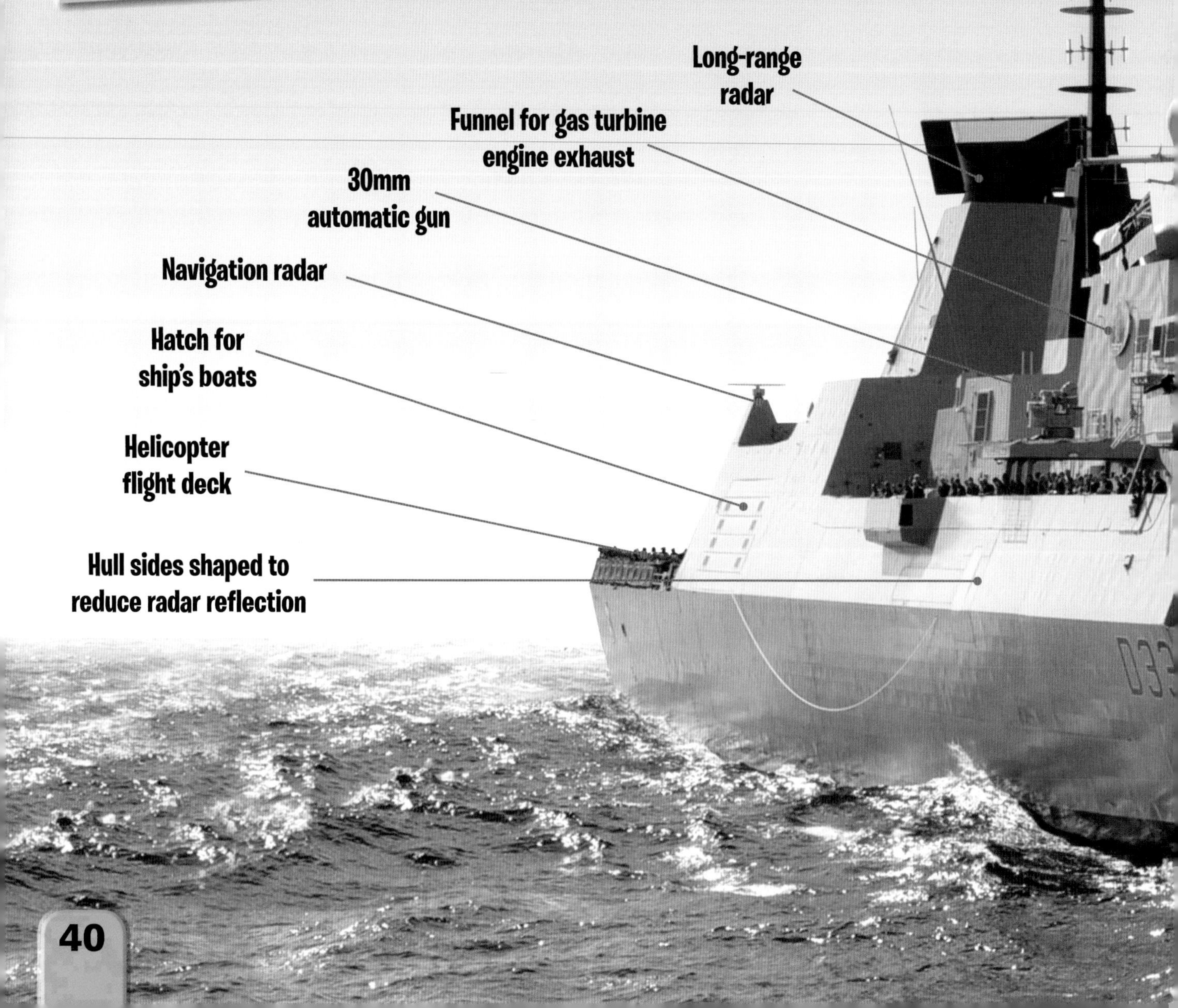

Long-range radar

Funnel for gas turbine engine exhaust

30mm automatic gun

Navigation radar

Hatch for ship's boats

Helicopter flight deck

Hull sides shaped to reduce radar reflection

D33

Communications mast

Sampson multi-function radar

Foremast

Navigation bridge

Minigun for close-in protection

TYPE 45 DESTROYER FACTS

Electric power
The Type 45 is driven by electric motors, which are powered by diesel generators and jet engines.

Smaller crew
The crew is about 190 sailors - 80 fewer than the previous Royal Navy destroyer.

Room for more
In addition to the crew, there's room to carry a force of up to 60 marines.

Super-sharp radar
The radar system can track an object smaller than a tennis ball approaching at three times the speed of sound!

Missiles to the sky
Up to 48 Sea Viper anti-aircraft missiles are carried in vertical launch tubes.

High spy
The foremast is very high to give the radar the furthest view possible - about 250 miles (400km).

Vertical launcher for Sea Viper missiles

4.5in calibre gun in "stealth" turret

Anchor

NAVY DIVER

Navy divers search underwater for mines that sink ships. When they find a mine they attach an explosive charge to destroy it - or call in a drone to do the job. They also clear obstacles, check ships for damage, recover sunken objects and look for enemy divers.

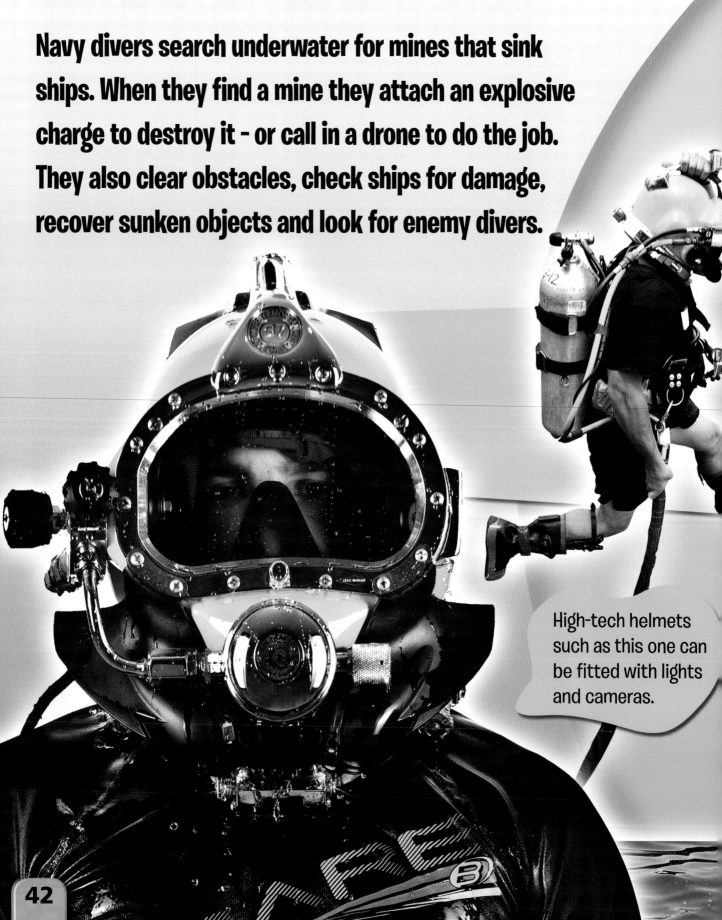

High-tech helmets such as this one can be fitted with lights and cameras.

DEADLY MINE

Sea mines come in all shapes and sizes. Some float free while others are tethered to the bottom like this one being inspected by a diver. Contact mines detonate when their spikes strike a ship and influence mines are triggered by noise or magnetic field disturbance.

BOOTS AND BRACES

This diver has weighted boots and is tethered to the dock, so he can't swim too far or go too deep. The equipment he is using is suited to working under ships and around structures on a harbour bottom.

DOLPHIN

The US Navy trains dolphins to search for mines. These divers don't need sophisticated equipment - they just use their natural echolocation ability to detect possible mines, and release a buoy to mark where they are. They can also spot and mark enemy frogmen divers.

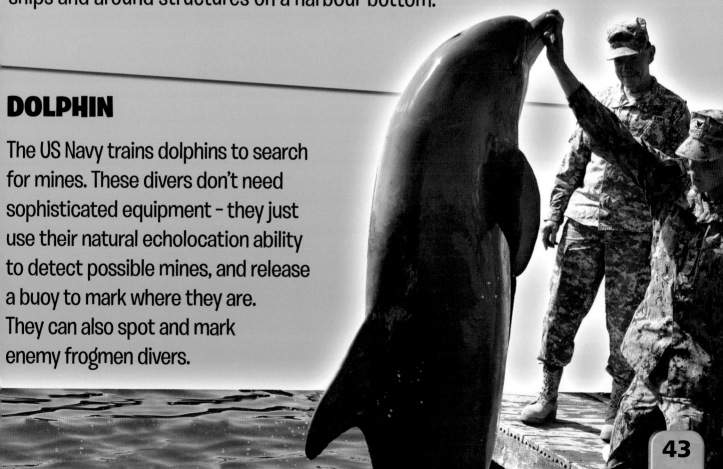

SUBMARINER

All modern submarines - be they ballistic missile launchers or attack submarines armed with torpedoes - use stealth, hiding beneath the waves. That's why submariners, who proudly wear their double dolphin insignia, call themselves the "Silent Service".

FIRE ONE!

With four torpedo tubes and 24 missile tubes, the new Virginia class is America's most powerful attack submarine. Each one costs $1.8 billion and takes seven years to build.

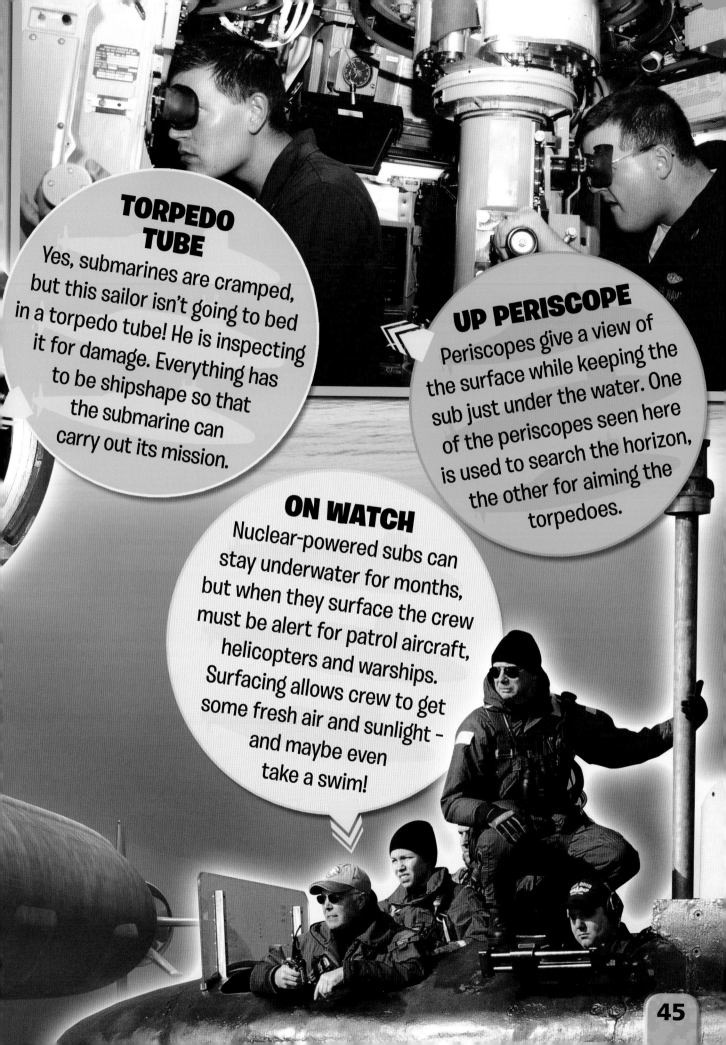

TORPEDO TUBE

Yes, submarines are cramped, but this sailor isn't going to bed in a torpedo tube! He is inspecting it for damage. Everything has to be shipshape so that the submarine can carry out its mission.

UP PERISCOPE

Periscopes give a view of the surface while keeping the sub just under the water. One of the periscopes seen here is used to search the horizon, the other for aiming the torpedoes.

ON WATCH

Nuclear-powered subs can stay underwater for months, but when they surface the crew must be alert for patrol aircraft, helicopters and warships. Surfacing allows crew to get some fresh air and sunlight – and maybe even take a swim!

LANDING SIGNAL OFFICER & FLIGHT DECK CREW

Getting aircraft safely on and off aircraft carriers is hard work in a harsh and dangerous environment. The deck crew are highly trained. Everyone wears a colour-coded jacket depending on their job and knows their place in the system.

An LSO talks a Super Hornet pilot through to another safe arrested landing or "trap" on the carrier.

BLUESHIRTS

Every time an aircraft stops on deck, Blueshirts chain it down and chock the wheels so it doesn't roll overboard or into another object.

LSO

The Landing Signal Officers (LSOs) guide aircraft to a carrier landing through radio calls and a special lighting system. Although they no longer wave bats so the pilots can follow their arm movements, these officers are still known as "Paddles".

YELLOWSHIRTS

The Yellowshirts direct aircraft movements, supervise catapult and arresting gear operations and give the final order to launch aircraft.

NIMITZ-CLASS AIRCRAFT CARRIER

America's Nimitz-class aircraft carriers are the largest warships ever built. With nearly 80 combat aircraft aboard, each one can deliver long-range strikes and reconnaissance missions, and defend itself against attacks.

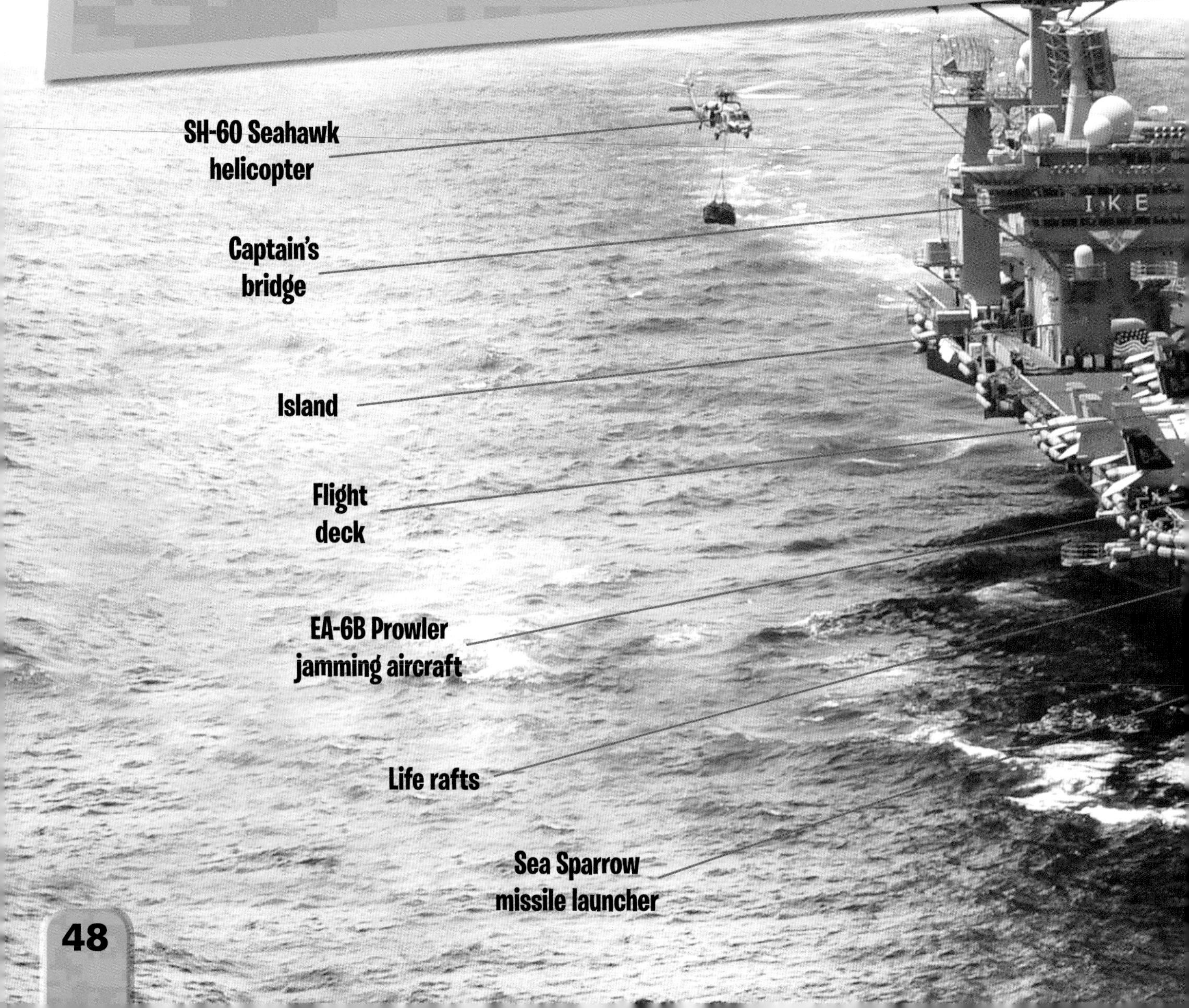

SH-60 Seahawk helicopter

Captain's bridge

Island

Flight deck

EA-6B Prowler jamming aircraft

Life rafts

Sea Sparrow missile launcher

NIMITZ-CLASS AIRCRAFT CARRIER FACTS

Big ship, big bucks
Each carrier costs around $4.5 billion (nearly £3 billion) - and that's not including the aircraft it carries.

Crowded carrier
A Nimitz-class carrier has a crew of nearly 5,500, including ship and air wing personnel.

Power station
The reactors generate enough electricity to power a city of 100,000 people.

Flat top
The flight deck is enormous - 1,092ft (333m) long, and around 4.5 acres (1.8 hectares) in area.

Fastest in the fleet
It has a top speed of over 35mph, faster than most smaller warships.

Long endurance
The carrier can run for up to 20 years on just one load of nuclear fuel.

Communications antennae

Radar

F/A-18C Hornet

E-2 Hawkeye early warning aircraft

Primary flight control

Aircraft catapult

F/A-18F Super Hornet

HH-60G PAVE HAWK HELICOPTER

The US Air Force's Pave Hawk finds personnel who are trapped behind enemy lines, goes in fast, picks them up and gets out quickly.

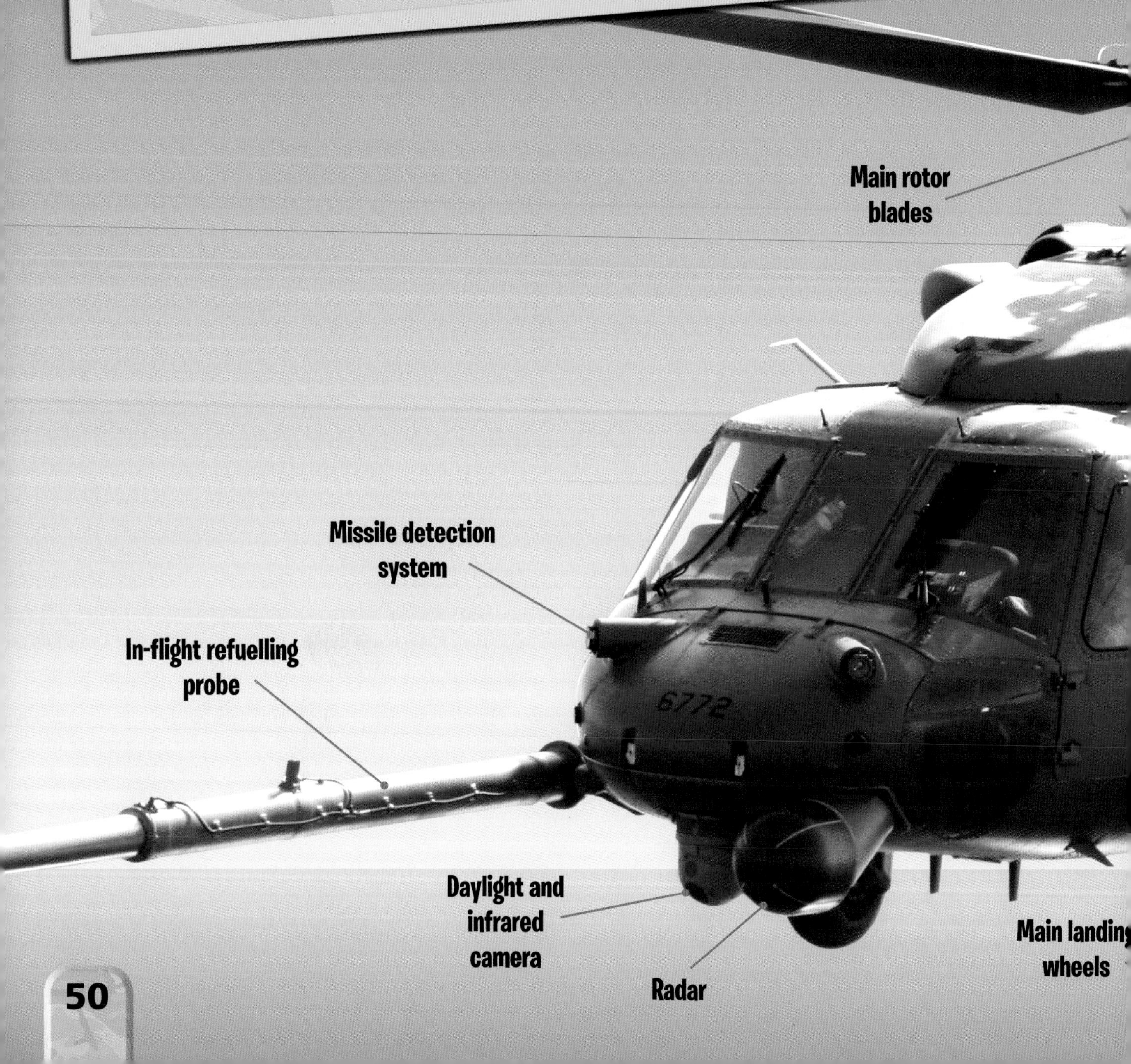

Main rotor blades

Missile detection system

In-flight refuelling probe

Daylight and infrared camera

Radar

Main landing wheels

6772

HH-60G PAVE HAWK HELICOPTER FACTS

Missile alert
A warning system looks for the flame of a launched missile and alerts the crew.

Fast escape
The HH-60G can accelerate to 185mph (298km/h) to get out of danger.

Firepower
Heavy guns are carried to defend the Pave Hawk during a rescue.

"Jolly Green Giant"
Its nickname, from the American War in Vietnam - when rescue copters were green.

Rescue ropes
The crew can lower a rope, a stretcher, a sling, a rope ladder or a "jungle penetrator" to pick up a survivor.

Motto
"These things we do, that others may live".

Infrared missile jammer

Turbine engine (one of two)

Tail rotor with four blades

Horizontal stabiliser (tailplane)

Missile radar jammer

Self-defence machine gun

Tail wheel

RESCUE HELICOPTER CREW

The Pave Hawk has a crew of up to six. There are two pilots, two Special Mission Operators, and two pararescue specialists - also called para jumpers or PJs. Together they stand ready to fly behind enemy lines on hazardous rescue missions.

This is what a Special Mission Operator from the USAF's 55th Rescue Squadron wears to work.

Mount for night-vision goggles

Helmet with face prote[...]

Microph[...] cable

Survival vest with pouches for first aid kit, signal mirror and flares, radio, compass, torch, GPS and pistol ammunition

Fireproof Nomex gloves

Survival knife pocket

Steel-toed flying boots

PILOT

Pave Hawk pilots are specially trained to fly at night and at low level to evade detection and enemy fire. They also train to land aboard ships and refuel the helicopter in-flight.

SPECIAL OPERATOR

The Special Mission Operators, sometimes also called flight engineers, are experts in the helicopter's systems. They operate the rescue hoist, fix mechanical problems and fire the door guns.

PARA JUMPER

The para jumpers leave the safety of the helicopter to look for downed aircrew, prove who they are and help them aboard. They have training in emergency medical techniques and survival in the field.

FIGHTER PILOT

It takes more training to become a fighter pilot than any other military job. US Navy pilots also have to learn to land and take off from aircraft carriers. No wonder they regard themselves as the very best.

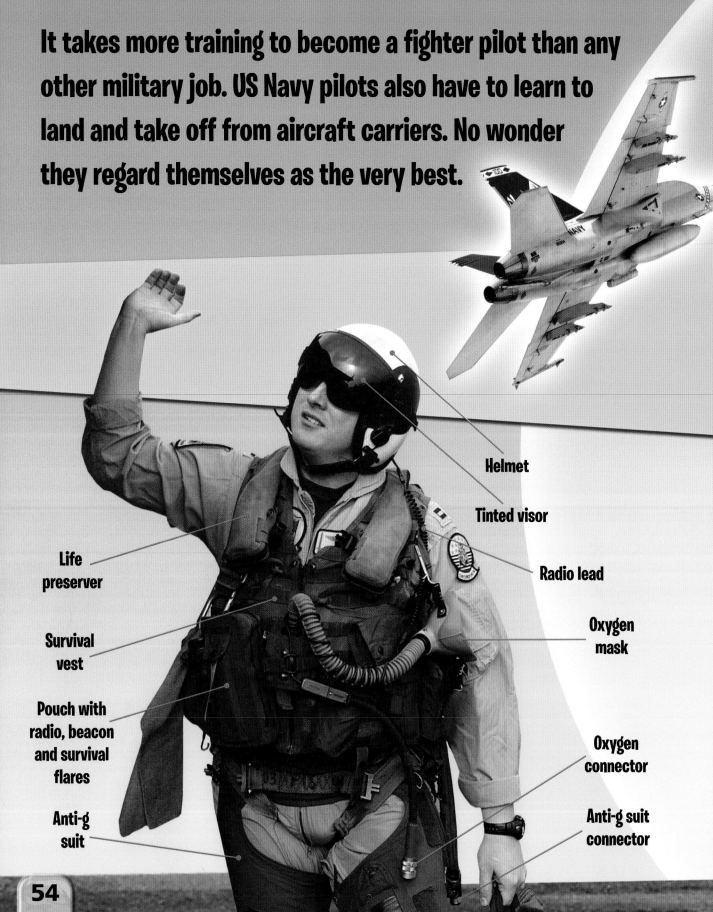

Helmet

Tinted visor

Radio lead

Oxygen mask

Oxygen connector

Anti-g suit connector

Life preserver

Survival vest

Pouch with radio, beacon and survival flares

Anti-g suit

HOT SEAT

In an emergency, the only way out might be to eject. Jet pilots sit on a rocket-powered ejection seat that can shoot them clear of a damaged jet in an instant. It's not a ride you want to take for fun.

DOGFIGHT

Pilots need good eyesight and must keep their heads turning in air combat to spot and follow enemy planes. Even with modern guided missiles, fighter pilots practise air combat manoeuvring or "dogfighting".

HIGH-TECH HELMET

New generation helmets do more than protect a pilot's head. An F-35 pilot's helmet projects images from the radar and cameras around the aircraft in front of his eyes. He can even "see" through the floor!

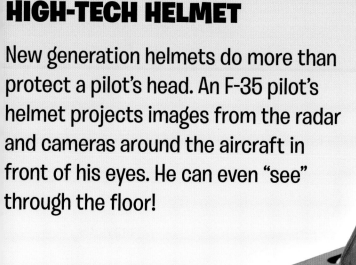

F/A-18E SUPER HORNET

The Super Hornet is the US Navy's primary fighter and attack aircraft. It can perform air defence and escort missions, attack ground targets and refuel other planes. It has replaced several other aircraft including the famous F-14 Tomcat.

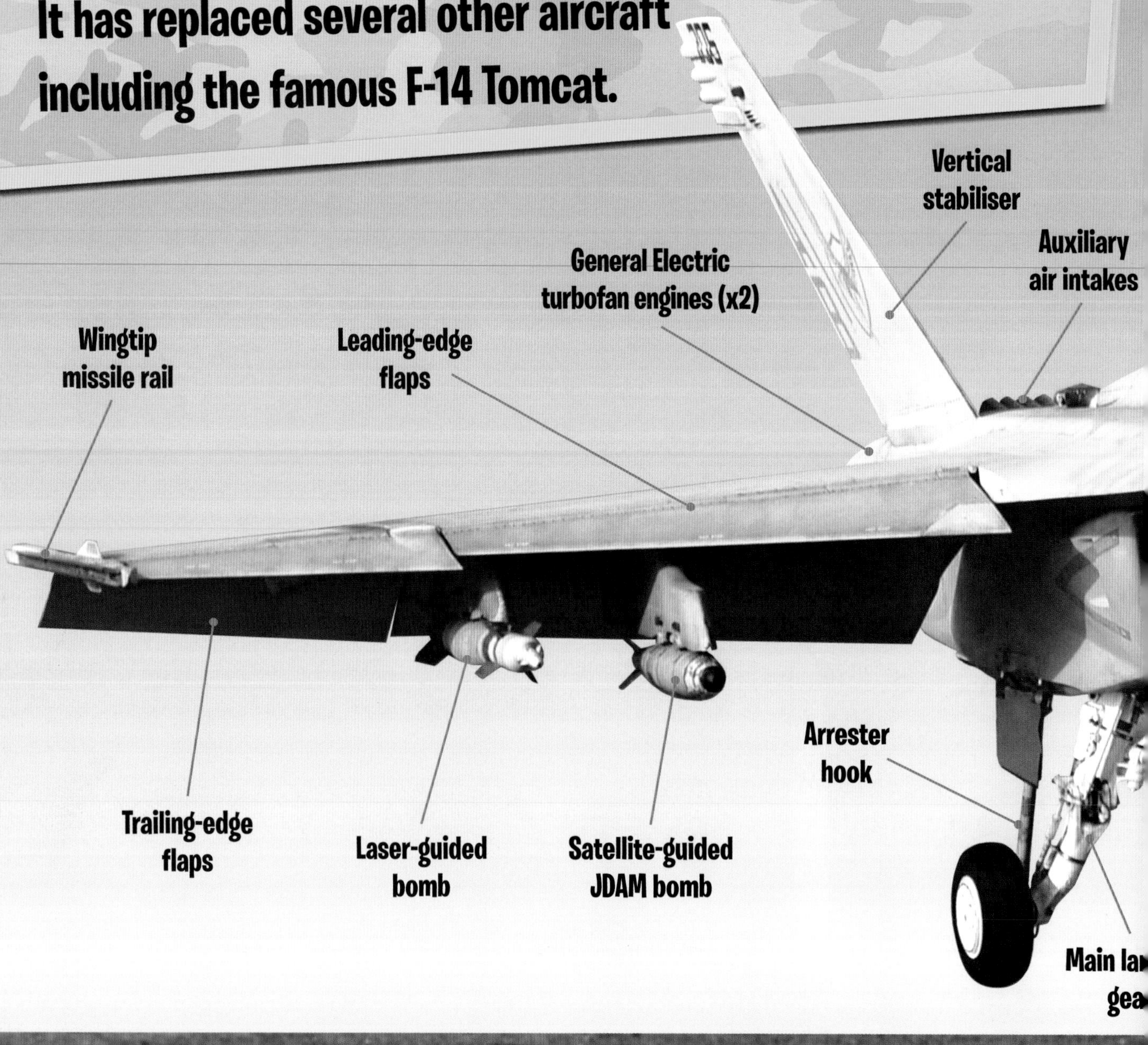

Vertical stabiliser

Auxiliary air intakes

General Electric turbofan engines (x2)

Wingtip missile rail

Leading-edge flaps

Trailing-edge flaps

Laser-guided bomb

Satellite-guided JDAM bomb

Arrester hook

Main landing gear

F/A-18E SUPER HORNET FACTS

Super models
The Super Hornet comes in single- and two-seat models, and in an electronic warfare version.

Radar resistant
Special surfaces and air intakes make the plane harder to detect with radar.

Bigger sting
The Super Hornet is about 25 per cent bigger and much more capable than the previous Hornet.

Fast and strong
An F/A-18E can travel nearly twice the speed of sound and carry more than its own weight.

Sailing away
The US Navy flies Super Hornets from its aircraft carriers; Australia has some too.

Bang for bucks
A Super Hornet costs about $57 million (£37.5 million). The new F-35 Lightning II costs twice as much.

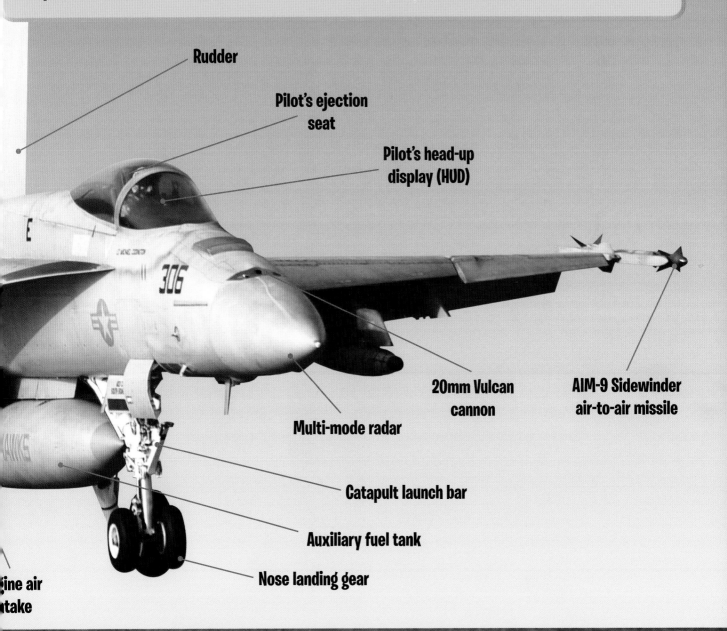

Rudder

Pilot's ejection seat

Pilot's head-up display (HUD)

20mm Vulcan cannon

AIM-9 Sidewinder air-to-air missile

Multi-mode radar

Catapult launch bar

Auxiliary fuel tank

Nose landing gear

Engine air intake

AIRCRAFT MAINTAINER

For every hour a warplane flies, hard-working men and women on the ground spend many more servicing its engines, fixing technical problems, loading weapons and generally making sure it is ready to go.

CHECK THE OIL

The maintainer's job goes on long after the flight crew has finished for the day. The C airlifter has four engines and many other parts that need inspecting before the next day's flying.

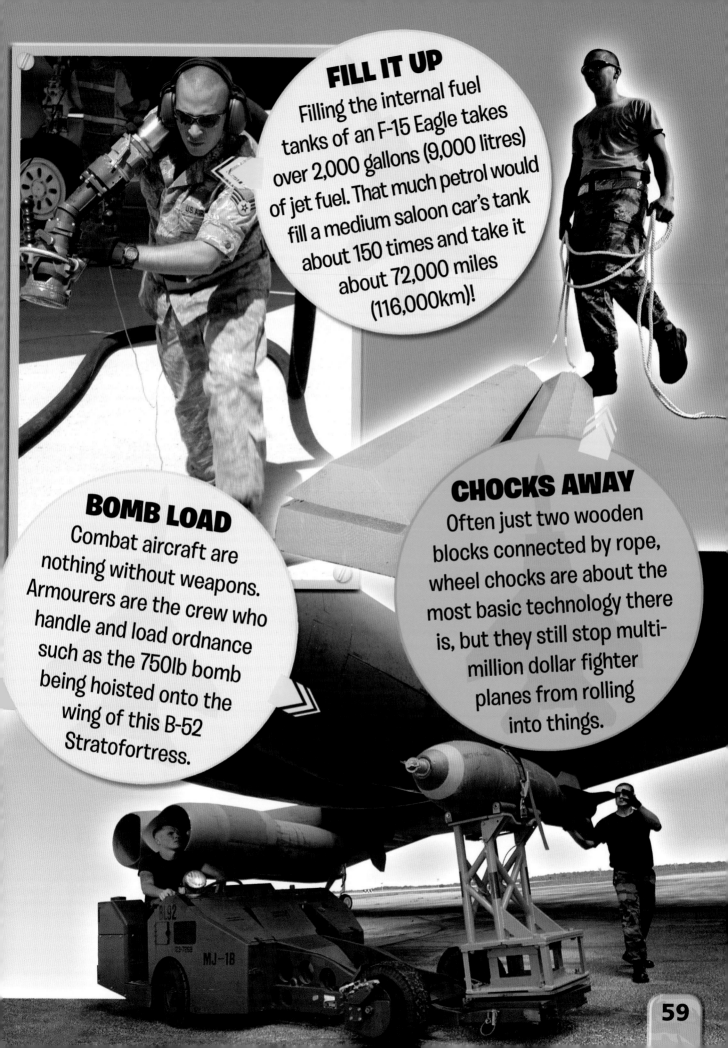

FILL IT UP

Filling the internal fuel tanks of an F-15 Eagle takes over 2,000 gallons (9,000 litres) of jet fuel. That much petrol would fill a medium saloon car's tank about 150 times and take it about 72,000 miles (116,000km)!

BOMB LOAD

Combat aircraft are nothing without weapons. Armourers are the crew who handle and load ordnance such as the 750lb bomb being hoisted onto the wing of this B-52 Stratofortress.

CHOCKS AWAY

Often just two wooden blocks connected by rope, wheel chocks are about the most basic technology there is, but they still stop multi-million dollar fighter planes from rolling into things.

CEREMONIAL

While combat soldiers will march in their best dress uniforms, most countries also have units, bands and mascots whose full-time job is ceremonial. They help to maintain traditions and remind the public of military history.

SILENT DRILL – WATCH THOSE BAYONETS!

The US Army's Silent Drill Team shows off precise skills based on old rifle-handling drills. They do it without shouting orders, as their name suggests – but with flying rifles!

THE BAND

Drums, horns, bagpipes and other instruments have been used for centuries to rally troops on the battlefield and spur them on. Military musicians still play traditional marches and other tunes today, but mainly at ceremonies and concerts.

ON PARADE

Here's an old tradition: a senior officer inspects the troops, in this case Welsh Guardsmen. Every boot, buckle and button is polished, medals arranged and rifle drill practised until everything is perfect.

MASCOT

Some units keep a mascot animal that appears at parades. These pampered creatures raise morale and help a unit to bond. Dogs and goats are popular, but military mascots include rams, ponies, birds of prey and even a penguin!

CANNON

A special occasion may call for a gun salute with historic artillery pieces or cannon. Up to 41 blank shells may be fired to salute dignitaries, mark commemorations or celebrate national days.

61

TRAINING
& TECHNIQUES

MARINE CORPS BOOT CAMP

Every recruit's training includes a "Boot Camp" - a period of intense physical trials. The Royal Marines' Commando course ends with a week of extra-tough tests, while US Marines endure 12 gruelling weeks of Boot Camp, topped off with a 54-hour field challenge.

WAR PAINT

Face paint is a skill of camouflage and concealment. Recruits learn to use colours and textures to stay hidden. They also learn ways to move and places to hide, such as keeping to the shadows.

MILITARY COMPASS

Soldiers learn to use a compass to navigate. Military compasses are waterproof, shock- and sand-proof.

HARD WORK

One aim of basic training is to build fitness. In addition to running and press-ups, recruits tackle assault courses to develop their stamina and teamwork skills.

GETTING DIRTY

Boot Camp includes tough challenges of endurance. Trainees must perform mud-crawls in full gear, often under obstacles such as barbed wire and at night!

MARTIAL ARTS

Recruits learn hand-to-hand combat including martial arts. The pugil stick is a padded pole-like baton that has been used in military training since World War II.

THE CRUCIBLE

In their final weeks of training, every recruit must take a 54-hour test before they can graduate as a US Marine. Known as "the Crucible", it's a super-tough series of obstacle courses, marches and battle exercises simulating a combat resupply mission.

MARCH

These recruits show the exhaustion of two-and-a-half days and nights of constant challenges. With little food or sleep, they still have one last exercise – a 10-mile (16km) march.

FIGHT

An assault course with weapons, smoke and simulated casualties tests the core military skills that the recruits have learned, including carrying a "wounded" buddy to safety.

CRAWL

Recruits must crawl through mud and water and under barbed wire. They may even have to form a bridge so that others can walk over them.

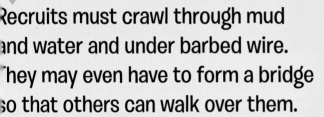

CLIMB

There are several courses to complete, with obstacles such as walls, rope nets and pipes to climb over or through. Carrying a barrel over a rope bridge is one exercise that needs teamwork.

JUNGLE SURVIVAL

The jungle is a hard place for conventional armies. As as well as the enemy, they have to contend with heat, high humidity, thick foliage, swollen rivers and creepy crawlies! This is why several armies run schools to train their forces in jungle operations.

WATER WADE

Exercises such as this group river walk help a unit to really come together as a team. A jungle patrol can't afford to forget or lose anyone, so they must all work together.

GATHER ROUND THE FIRE
At the Jungle Warfare Training Center on the island of Okinawa, Japan, US Marines wait for another lesson. The basic jungle skills course lasts five days, ending in an endurance test on the sixth.

CRITTERS
Snakes and scorpions can be as deadly as enemy weapons and booby traps, but if you know how to handle them, and know which ones aren't dangerous, they are not so frightening.

WHERE NEXT?
With no paths and landmarks, and the sun often hidden, jungle navigation often requires relearning basic map and compass skills to find the objective and get out again.

JUNGLE WARFARE

In the jungle or other tropical environment, visibility may be restricted to short distances, heavy weapons can't easily be used, and vehicles are restricted to what few roads there are. Jungle terrain favours guerrillas and insurgent forces who know how to live off the land.

ANY WAY THAT WORKS, EVEN IF IT'S WET

Moving quietly and keeping their weapons dry, New Zealand soldiers wade through a swamp. Let's just hope there are no snakes under there...

ROPE DOES THE TRICK

When the forest is too thick for a helicopter to land, the only way in may be by sliding down a rope. Heavy jungle can only be patrolled on foot

SPEED AND COVER

Combat in the jungle will likely be at close quarters and may break out suddenly. This Australian soldier on exercise in the Solomon Islands is using the cover of trees and foliage to move safely.

SURVIVAL KIT

A soldier who gets separated from his platoon could save his life with the things in this small kit, which includes a wire saw, insect repellent, antiseptic ointment, firelighters, fishing line and a compass.

COLD WEATHER TRAINING

Military operations happen all year round, and in some places winter conditions last most of the year. Cold weather can be as dangerous to soldiers as bombs and bullets. Soldiers must learn to live and fight when the temperature is well below freezing.

BRRRRRRR!

This man has just spent five minutes in a freezing Alaskan river and is now trying to warm up using simple techniques - such as sheltering in the relative warmth of a shared two-man tent.

CHOPPER

For helicopter pilots, snow landings take extra training. Blowing snow can make the landing spot invisible, and wheeled helicopters can sink up to their bellies.

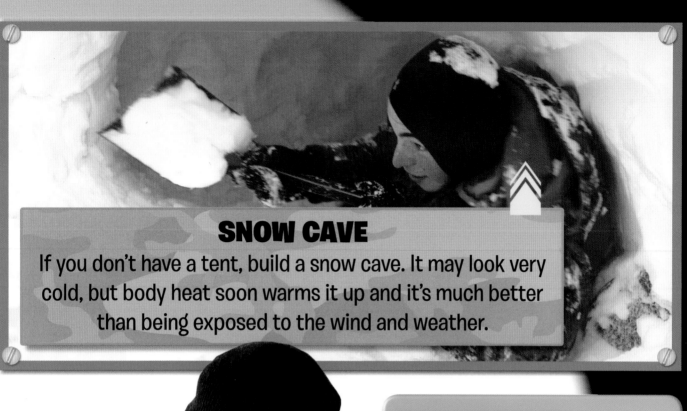

SNOW CAVE

If you don't have a tent, build a snow cave. It may look very cold, but body heat soon warms it up and it's much better than being exposed to the wind and weather.

COOKING HOT

Just because it is cold and you are outdoors doesn't mean you can't have a hot meal, even Mexican food. Hearty food is essential for working hard in cold climates.

ESSENTIAL SHELTER

Knocking in a tent peg in frozen ground is just one of the challenges of cold weather, but putting up a shelter for the night is vital.

COLD WEATHER OPERATIONS

Mountain warfare and cold weather fighting put a strain on both man and machine. Equipment freezes up or just doesn't work as well. High altitude saps strength and affects weapons accuracy. Visibility can be poor and movement difficult, but the right gear gets the mission done.

SNOW PATROL

These soldiers are dealing with a treacherous environment - deep snow in mountainous terrain.

MOUNTAIN MORTAR

US Army troops fire a mortar from a base high up in a mountain range. At higher altitudes, projectiles have different flight paths than they do at sea level, making aiming harder.

WRAP UP WARM

There's no such thing as bad weather, just bad clothing, some people say. Falling snow and poor visibility are no problem for a soldier with the right equipment.

SNOW CAT

This personnel carrier was designed in Sweden for snow conditions. It has wide rubber tracks, which give a low ground-pressure "footprint". The troops travel in a trailer at the back.

TANK SCHOOL

The Armor School, now at Fort Benning, Georgia, is the main training centre for US Army crews on the Abrams tank and the Bradley Infantry Fighting Vehicle. US Marines and foreign students also train here to operate and maintain the Abrams.

SIMULATOR

This odd-looking compartment is an Abrams driving simulator. It shows how little room the driver has in the real thing. The reclined seat is said to be the most comfortable one in the tank.

MANOEUVRE AS ONE

In combat, tanks work in groups. Commanders and crews must learn to operate their tanks together for mutual protection and best combat effectiveness.

HOME ON THE RANGE

Accurate and fast firing wins a tank battle. To graduate, Abrams crews must demonstrate they can repeatedly hit targets at long-range, both while moving and stationary, in strict time limits.

MAINTENANCE

The Abrams tank needs loving care at the depot and in the field. This complex machine is powered by a jet engine and is full of computer technology, so there's a lot to teach technicians and crews about its maintenance.

BRADLEY

The M2 Bradley is an infantry fighting vehicle - an armoured personnel carrier with a 25mm cannon. The Armor School teaches Bradley crews how to work with the infantry they carry into battle.

TANK OPERATIONS

Tanks provide mobile firepower and can destroy enemy vehicles at long ranges. Large tank battles are fairly rare today, but tanks can still play a crucial role on the battlefield, even in conflicts where the opposition has no tanks.

 ## NO OBSTACLE

Where other vehicles have to go around obstacles, tanks can go over them or through them (though they can still get stuck!). This Canadian Leopard is crossing a *wadi,* or water channel.

NIGHT MOVES

Modern tanks such as the M1 have an advantage after dark. They have superior night sights and thermal vision equipment which help their crews see older enemy tanks and vehicles long before they are detected themselves.

NECESSARY POWER

US tanks fire at an insurgent target. Although some people think tanks are becoming a thing of the past, heavy armour is useful for destroying fortifications while remaining well protected from most weapons.

PLOUGH ON

By using front-mounted plough blades (such as those seen at the bottom here), a tank can tip over land mines and IEDs. The Abrams can also be fitted with a bulldozer blade to clear earth barriers and other obstructions, or a mine roller to detonate mines away from the tank.

PEACEKEEPING

The United Nations, NATO and other organisations ask member states to send troops overseas for peacekeeping missions, to prevent conflict or stop it restarting. Peacekeepers keep warring groups apart and ensure that aid supplies and health services reach the local population.

BLUE BERET, BLUE HELMET

A peace treaty or ceasefire between warring groups or nations may need to be enforced by others. The UN's peacekeepers wear blue berets or helmets and drive white vehicles as symbols of their neutrality.

HELPING HAND

In a war-torn area, shipments of food and humanitarian supplies for the people require delivering and protecting. Sometimes soldiers do this, but mainly they escort aid convoys and keep the distribution point safe.

OPEN IMMEDIATE

LAND MINE LEGACY

Mines are left behind after many conflicts. They must be cleared, or at least mapped, before civilians can return to their villages and farms. It can sometimes take years to make an area completely safe.

WALL OF THANKS

Grateful locals painted this wall with the flags of nations in KFOR, the Kosovo Force run by NATO. A peacekeeping force may be needed for a long time after major fighting stops - in this case, since 1999.

RIOT RESPONSE

Peacekeepers sometimes work in tense environments and have to deal with angry crowds - even riots. Quick intervention is the key to limiting disturbances and preventing violence spreading.

CAMOUFLAGE

Camouflage is the art of concealment, of blending into the background so that you can barely be seen. On the battlefield, the use of the right colours or the right foliage can make the difference between being almost undetectable and sticking out like a sore thumb!

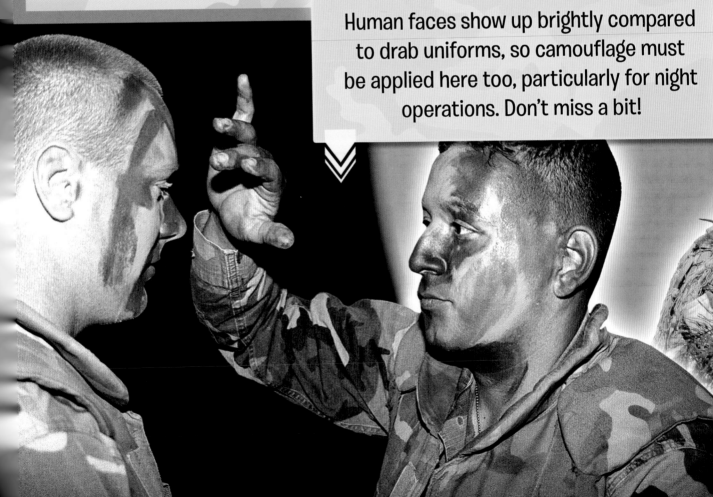

FACE PAINT

Human faces show up brightly compared to drab uniforms, so camouflage must be applied here too, particularly for night operations. Don't miss a bit!

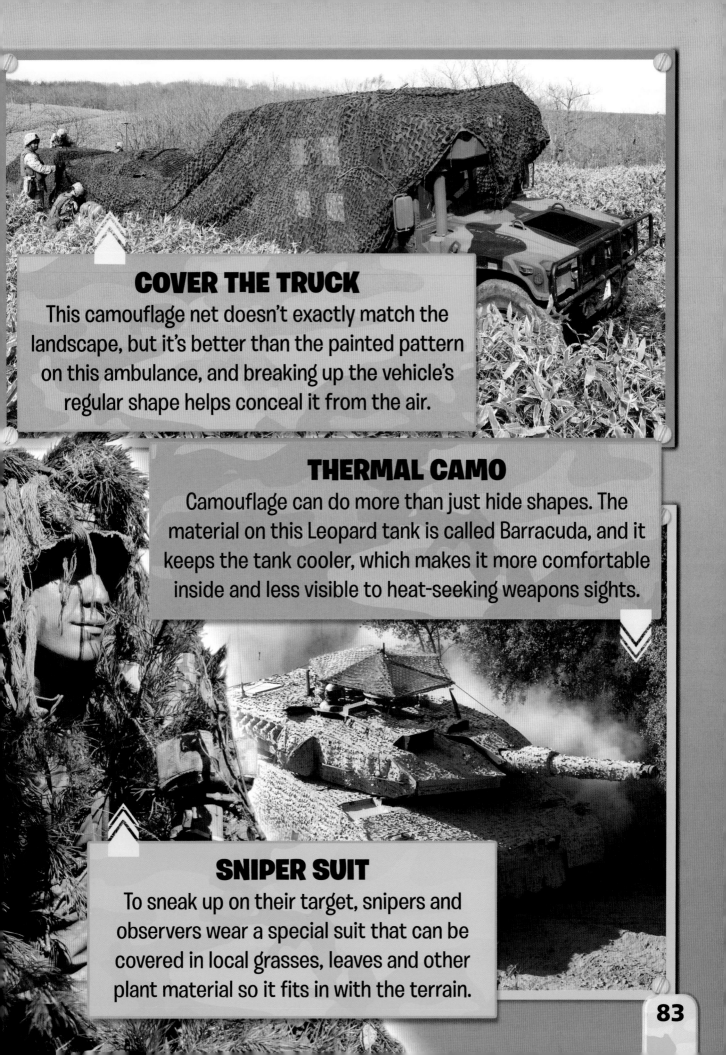

COVER THE TRUCK

This camouflage net doesn't exactly match the landscape, but it's better than the painted pattern on this ambulance, and breaking up the vehicle's regular shape helps conceal it from the air.

THERMAL CAMO

Camouflage can do more than just hide shapes. The material on this Leopard tank is called Barracuda, and it keeps the tank cooler, which makes it more comfortable inside and less visible to heat-seeking weapons sights.

SNIPER SUIT

To sneak up on their target, snipers and observers wear a special suit that can be covered in local grasses, leaves and other plant material so it fits in with the terrain.

URBAN TRAINING

Cities and towns are very difficult places to patrol or control; movement is restricted and there are hundreds of places for enemies to hide. This is why many armies create whole mock towns and villages, with buildings, markets and even actors playing roles, to help soldiers be better prepared.

VILLAGE PEOPLE
This market looks calm, but an "attack" could happen at any moment, so trainees must learn to stay fully alert.

PEOPLE SKILLS
Training with actors standing in as locals can help soldiers be more sensitive in real life situations. These young children are very happy to play ball.

NECESSARY FORCE

You can't always afford to be polite in a bad neighbourhood. Searches for insurgents or hidden weapons sometimes need doors to be opened with mallets or even explosives.

AROUND THE CORNER

Every door and alleyway may hide an enemy. Entering a room must be done carefully, with back-up from troops behind.

URBAN OPERATIONS

The last few decades have seen urban fighting in many places. Urban warfare gets called funny names, such as FIBUA (Fighting In Built-Up Areas) and FISH (Fighting In Somebody's House), but it's a very serious business for both soldiers and local residents alike.

MARINES ON PATROL

Security patrols in occupied cities are both essential and extremely hazardous. These Marines have to be totally alert to potential attacks, while making sure they do not harm the local citizens who pose no threat.

CHECKPOINT DUTY

When taking charge of an urban area, it's vital that traffic in and out is monitored and controlled. To do this job, a soldier needs to be alert to any dangers - and very patient.

MAKING CONTACT

Translators and liaison officers can make a big difference. Children are victims of war too; a little care and compassion goes a long way.

 ## HEARTS AND MINDS

Winning the trust of the locals is vital once the fighting stops. Reaching out to children helps reassure citizens.

SPECIAL FORCES
HOSTAGE RESCUE TRAINING

Enemy forces, terrorists or disturbed people sometimes take innocent people as hostages. These are very tricky situations, so Special Forces are highly trained in entering buildings, defeating hostage-takers and then rescuing people unharmed.

AIRLINER ASSAULT

A night-vision image shows a Special Forces team member training in a disused airliner. With many people in a confined space, hijacked aircraft situations require extra care.

STACKED

When searching a larger building, Special Forces work in groups or "stacks" of four, with each man covering one direction from possible threats.

SHOOT HOUSE

Rooms made of plywood stand in for a building where hostages are hidden. Commandos can practise entering rooms, finding the hostage, dealing with the hostage-takers and withdrawing safely.

ROOM CLEARED

Special Forces don't mess around. Speed of action, lots of noise and even a scary appearance can all help resolve a situation in a few moments without friendly casualties.

DON'T COME ANY CLOSER!

These two soldiers are playing the part of a hostage-taker and his captive. The authorities must decide quickly what to do: agree to his demands? Try to talk him into giving up? Use force?

AIRCREW
WATER SURVIVAL TRAINING

In case their aeroplane or helicopter crashes in water or they have to parachute into the sea, navy pilots and aircrew undergo water survival training. They take a series of tests every four years - in full flying gear. It's a case of sink or swim!

INTO THE POOL AGAIN

Pilots have to demonstrate swimming in full flying suit, parachute harness and boots. The helmet actually helps them stay afloat, but they won't break any Olympic records in the pool.

SWET BOX

The Shallow Water Egress Trainer (SWET) tips the pilot upside down while he or she tries to unbuckle a seat belt. Although the pilot can breathe from a small air bottle, a lot of water goes up the nose!

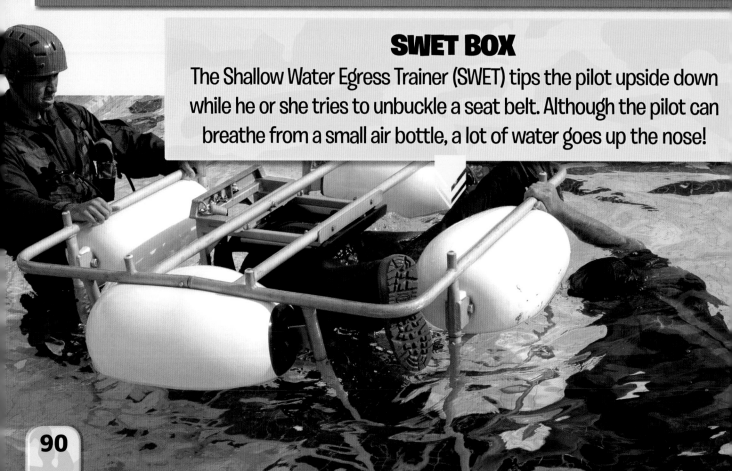

DUNK TANK

The Helo Dunker stands in for a helicopter cabin. It is dropped in a pool and turned over as it sinks. The passengers have to unstrap themselves, escape the Dunker, reach the surface and then swim a length of the pool.

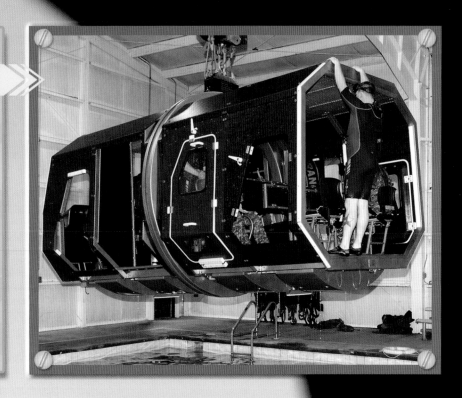

WHAT A DRAG

Even after a safe sea landing, a parachute may drag the pilot through the water. This exercise teaches them to release a chute before he or she swallows too much ocean.

WET AND WILD

Training continues outdoors. Getting eight men into a life raft is tricky even in calm waters. Don't throw away your helmet - you might need it for bailing out the raft!

GLOSSARY

AIRCRAFT CARRIER
A ship with a flight deck for landing aeroplanes

AIRLIFTER
A transport aircraft for moving troops and equipment

AMBUSH
A surprise attack

AMPHIBIOUS OPERATION
Landing troops and equipment from ships to the shore

ANTI-PERSONNEL MINE
A bomb triggered by being stepped on

ANTI-TANK MINE
A bomb set off by a tank or vehicle driving over it

ARMOURED PERSONNEL CARRIER (APC)
A wheeled or tracked vehicle for transporting troops

ARTILLERY
Heavy guns that fire long-range shells

BOOT CAMP
An ultra-tough training course - such as the one taken by US Marines (below)

BUTTONED UP
Tankers' term that means a tank's hatches are all closed

CANNON
A machine gun that fires explosive shells,

CLOSE AIR SUPPORT
Air attacks on targets that are near friendly troops

COMMANDOS
Soldiers trained to carry out raids

CONVOY
A group of vehicles or ships travelling together

CRUCIBLE
The final exercise in a US Marine's basic training

DESTROYER
A class of warship between frigate and cruiser

ELECTRONIC WARFARE
Using electronic systems to jam, deceive or neutralise the enemy's radios, radars and other equipment

ENGINEERS
Soldiers who build bridges, clear roads, etc.

FAC
Forward Air Controller - a soldier who calls in close air support aircraft to attack

FIGHTER
An aeroplane with the primary role of destroying enemy aircraft

FRIENDLY FIRE
A mistaken attack by a force on its own people or allie

FROGMAN
A combat diver

GPS
Global Positioning System

GRENADE
hand-thrown or rifle-fired explosive weapon

GUERILLAS
groups of soldiers using ambush attacks and IEDs to fight a regular army

HOWITZER
a type of heavy artillery that fires large shells at a steep angle

IED
improvised explosive device - a bomb usually made by terrorists or insurgents

IFV
Infantry Fighting Vehicle - an APC with a turret and cannon

INFANTRY
regular foot soldiers

INSIGNIA
symbols or emblems that show force, regiment or rank

INSURGENTS
soldiers fighting for a non-government army, often using guerilla tactics

JTAC
Joint Terminal Attack Controller - another term for FAC

LAND MINE
a bomb that's left on the ground to be set off by being stepped on or driven over

LOGISTICS
Moving troops and supplying their equipment, ammunition and food

MACHINE GUN
a gun that fires continuously when the trigger is pulled

MARINES
soldiers specialising in amphibious operations

MBT
Main Battle Tank (right)

MEDEVAC
Medical evacuation of injured soldiers

MORTAR
A type of light artillery that fires small bombs at a steep angle

MRAP
Mine-Resistant Ambush-Protected vehicle

NCO
Non-Commissioned Officer - in the army, a corporal or sergeant

PARATROOPERS
Soldiers specialising in parachute landings

PEACEKEEPER
A soldier on a mission to enforce or monitor a ceasefire or prevent violence between groups

RECONNAISSANCE
Searching or observing an area for military purposes

RECRUIT
A new soldier, not yet trained

(WEAPON) SIGHT
A device used to aim weapons by eye or electronically

SAM
Surface to Air Missile

SNIPERS
Specially trained soldiers who use extremely accurate rifles to kill at a distance

SPECIAL FORCES
Soldiers with extra training using non-standard techniques, often on dangerous special missions

TANK
A heavily armoured vehicle with tracks and a large main gun

UAV
Unmanned Aerial Vehicle - a drone aircraft (right)

FURTHER INFORMATION

Visiting a museum is a great way to learn more about the armed forces.

United Kingdom

National Army Museum
The leading authority on the British Army; has a special Kids' Zone.
Royal Hospital Road, Chelsea, London SW3 4HT
www.nam.ac.uk

Imperial War Museum
This museum is dedicated to the understanding of war and warfare,
past and present, and often has exhibitions specially designed for children.
The IWM has five locations, including:
Lambeth Road, London SE1 6HZ
www.iwm.org.uk

National Museum of the Royal Navy
One of Britain's oldest maritime museums, telling the history of the Fleet.
HM Naval Base (PP66), Portsmouth, Hampshire PO1 3NH
www.royalnavalmuseum.org

Royal Air Force Museum
Two sites tell the story of the Royal Air Force; the largest is
Royal Air Force Museum London, Grahame Park Way, London, NW9 5LL
www.rafmuseum.org.uk

Canada

Canadian War Museum
Canada's national museum of military history, with an emphasis on peacekeeping
and current involvements.
1 Vimy Place, Ottawa, Ontario K1A 0M8
www.warmuseum.ca

United States

National Museum of the US Air Force
With over 300 aircraft and missiles on display, this is the official museum of the USAF
1100 Spaatz Street, Wright-Patterson, AFB OH 45433 (near Dayton)
www.nationalmuseum.af.mil

National Museum of the Marine Corps
Dedicated to the preservation and promotion of Marine Corps history and tradition.
18900 Jefferson Davis Hwy. Triangle, VA 22172
www.usmcmuseum.com

National Museum of the United States Navy
A collection of US Naval artefacts, with several sites, the largest being in Washington.
Washington Navy Yard, 805 Kidder Breese Street, SE Washington, DC 20374-5060
www.history.navy.mil/museums

Australia

Australian War Memorial
A museum dedicated to the memory of Australian servicemen who lost
their lives in the two World Wars. There's a children's Discovery Zone.
Treloar Crescent (top of ANZAC Parade), Campbell, ACT 2612, Australia
www.awm.gov.au

New Zealand

National Army Museum, Waiouru.
New Zealand's most comprehensive Army Museum, full of history and hardware
Corner State Highway One and Hassett Drive, Waiouru, New Zealand
www.armymuseum.co.nz

INDEX

PICTURE CREDITS

1	United States Marine Corps (USMC)
2-3	Defense Video and Imagery Distribution System (DVIDS)
4-5	4 top: USMC; bottom: AgustaWestland
	5 top: DVIDS; bottom: USMC
6-7	United States Navy (USN)
8-9	USMC
10-11	10 top: International Security Assistance Force (ISAF); bottom: Australian Department of Defence; 11 top: ISAF; bottom: US Army
12-13	All: USMC
14-15	All: DVIDS
16-17	14 both: DVIDS 15 top: Jim Winchester; bottom: DVIDS
18-19	18 both: US Army; right: 19 both: US Air Force (USAF)
20-21	20 both: USMC
	21 top: USAF; bottom: USMC; bottom left Defenselink; bottom right; USMC
22-23	DVIDS
24-25	24: USMC
	25 top: US Army; bottom left: USMC; bottom right: USN
26-27	26: Jim Winchester
	27 top: USMC; middle: DVIDS; bottom: Jim Winchester
28-29	Jim Winchester
30-31	30: USAF
	31 top: USMC; middle DVIDS; bottom Jim Winchester
32-33	Jim Winchester
34-35	34 top: via Robert Hewson; bottom: USMC
	35 top: Canadian Department of National Defence (DND); bottom: USN
36-37	36 top: US Army; bottom left: Jim Winchester; bottom right: USMC
	37 top left: USN; top right: ISAF; bottom: USN
38-39	38 left: USN; right: Jim Winchester
	39: top, bottom left: Jim Winchester; bottom right: USN
40-41	USN
42-43	42 left: DVIDS; right: USN
	43 top left: NATO; top right: DVIDS; bottom: USN
44-45	All: USN
46-47	46 top left and top right: USN; bottom: DVIDS
48-49	USN

50-51	55th RQS via Lt. Col. Bob Remey
52-53	52: 55th RQS via Lt. Col. Bob Remey
	53 top left: DVIDS; top right USAF; bottom DVIDS
54-55	54 left: USN; right: DVIDS
	55 left: DVIDS; right Jim Winchester; bottom: USN
56-57	USN
58-59	All: USAF
60-61	60 top: USMC; lower Defense Link
	61 top and middle: UK Ministry of Defence/ Crown Copyright; lower: USMC
62-63	US Army
64-65	64 top: Shutterstock; left: Aaron Amat/Thinkstock; right: iStockphoto/Thinkstock
	65 below left and right: Robert Nickelsberg/Getty Images
66-67	66: DVIDS 67: All USMC
68-69	68 top: USMC All others: DVIDS
70-71	70 top: UK MoD/Crown Copyright; bottom: New Zealand Defence Force
	71 left: USMC; right: Australian Defence Force; bottom: DVIDS
72-73	72 left: DVIDS; right: UK MoD/Crown Copyright
	73 top: DVIDS; bottom left: USAF; bottom right: USMC
74-75	74: USMC 75 top: DVIDS; others USMC
76-77	76 top: Defense Link; bottom: US Army Armor School
	77 top: US Army; middle and bottom: US Army Armor School
78-79	78: US Army 79 top: USAF middle and lower: USMC
80-81	80 top: DVIDS; bottom: KFOR
	81 top and bottom left: USMC; bottom right: Defenseimagery.mil
82-83	82 top: DVIDS; bottom USMC
	83 top and bottom left: USMC; bottom right: Saab Barracuda
84-85	84 top: USMC; bottom: DVIDS 85 all: USMC
86-87	86 top: Defenseimagery.mil; bottom Defense Link
	87 top: UK MOD/Crown Copyright; middle: Australian Defence Force; bottom: USMC
88-89	88 left: USAF; right: Australian Defence Force
	89 top: US Navy; others: USN
90-91	All: DVIDS
92-93	92 and 93: USMC
94-95	94 top: USAF middle: US Army
96	DVIDS

Background and incidental camouflage patterns sourced from www.vecteezy.com

Every effort has been made to trace the copyright holders, and we apologise in advance for any unintentional omissions. We would be pleased to insert the appropriate acknowledgements in any subsequent edition of this publication.